Ghost Hunter

VIRGINIA LOH-HAGAN

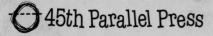

45th Parallel Press

Published in the United States of America by Cherry Lake Publishing
Ann Arbor, Michigan
www.cherrylakepublishing.com

Content Adviser: Chris Bailey & Kara Swanson, technical advisers, Grimstone Inc. Paranormal Investigators, Ypsilanti, Michigan
Reading Adviser: Marla Conn, ReadAbility, Inc.
Book Design: Felicia Macheske

Photo Credits: © Peter Kim/Shutterstock.com, cover, 1; © sebra/Shutterstock.com, 5; © Akos Nagy/Shutterstock.com, 8; © Peter Dedeurwaerder/Shutterstock.com, 9; © Carolyn Seelen/Dreamstime.com, 11; © inhauscreative/iStock, 13; © Passigatti/Dreamstime.com, 14-15; © Joseph Kaczmarek/ZUMAPRESS/Newscom, 17; © Everett Historical/Shutterstock.com; 19; © Steve Pering/Thinkstock, 20; © meshaphoto/iStock, 23; © Twin Design/Shutterstock.com; © Peter Dedeurwaerder/Shutterstock.com, 27; © Shane Maritch/Shutterstock.com, 28; © ARENA Creative/Shutterstock.com, cover and multiple interior pages; © oculo/Shutterstock.com, multiple interior pages; © Denniro/Shutterstock.com, multiple interior pages; © PhotoHouse/Shutterstock.com, multiple interior pages; © Miloje/Shutterstock.com, multiple interior pages

45th Parallel Press is an imprint of Cherry Lake Publishing.

Library of Congress Cataloging-in-Publication Data

Loh-Hagan, Virginia.
  Ghost hunter : odd jobs / Virginia Loh-Hagan.
     pages cm — (Odd jobs)
  Includes bibliographical references and index.
  ISBN 978-1-63470-028-3 (hardcover) — ISBN 978-1-63470-082-5 (pdf) — ISBN 978-1-63470-055-9 (pbk.) — ISBN 978-1-63470-109-9 (ebook)
  1. Ghosts—Research. I. Title.

  BF1471.L64 2016
  133.1—dc23

                    2015008261

Cherry Lake Publishing would like to acknowledge the work of The Partnership for 21st Century Skills. Please visit www.p21.org for more information.

Printed in the United States of America
Corporate Graphics Inc.

Contents

Who You Gonna Call?

What are guardian ghosts? What do people report about ghosts? Why do people call ghost hunters? How do ghost hunters help people?

Melba Goodwyn studies ghosts. Her grandson, Michael, saw a ghost.

The ghost was a boy. The ghost jumped on Michael's bed. The ghost did this for three nights. Michael's parents didn't believe him. He was scared. So he slept in the living room. That night, a car crashed into

Michael's room. Goodwyn thinks the ghost saved Michael's life.

Goodwyn believes in **guardian** ghosts. Guardians protect others. They warn people of danger. Goodwyn doesn't want people to be scared of ghosts.

Ghost hunters help us understand that ghosts can be good.

Each year, thousands of people report seeing ghosts. They report strange activities. They hear noises. They see strange lights. They feel cold air.

People are scared of the unknown. They call ghost hunters. Ghost hunters study the **paranormal**. Paranormal is anything to do with unexplained events.

Ghost hunters try to understand ghosts. They investigate **hauntings**. Hauntings are when a ghost bothers a person or thing. Ghost hunters are not **mediums**. They do not talk to ghosts.

Many people are scared of ghosts.

THAT HAPPENED?!?

Amy Bruni starred in *Ghost Hunters*. She joked about designing a kid's lunch box like a Ouija board. A Ouija board is used to talk to dead people. It was a Halloween joke. She didn't expect people to get mad. Somebody wrote to Bruni, "Ouija boards are NOT toys and should not be marketed to kids. ... Don't mess with it unless you want uninvited dark spirits invading your home and possessing your things and/or family." People were shocked and angry. Some people sent her death threats. Bruni said, "To those of you who have said terrible things about me because this joke went right over your head, I'd rather sleep on a bed of Ouija boards than associate with you anyway."

A cop in New Mexico watched a video. He saw a ghost. It was in a parking lot. It floated through a fence. The cop was scared.

Benjamin Radford has hunted ghosts for many years. He studied the video. He noticed the ghost didn't go through the fence. The ghost went over the fence. Also, the ghost was on the camera lens. The ghost was not a ghost. It was a bug.

Sometimes strange things have nothing to do with ghosts. Ghost hunters help people feel safe.

*Benjamin Radford has traveled the world. He has studied
ghosts, monsters, alien signals, and haunted houses.*

CHAPTER 2

Ghost Hunters and Research!

What do ghost hunters do? How are ghost hunters like scientists? How are ghost hunters like historians? How do ghost hunters work? What equipment do ghost hunters use?

Ghost hunters study haunted places. They often find simple reasons for strange sights and sounds.

A couple heard bangs. They saw shaky lights. They heard screams. Jason Hawes and Grant Wilson examined the house. They found squirrels. The squirrels banged in the walls. The screams came from a hawk. It was trapped in the attic. A loose wire made the lights flicker.

But sometimes ghost hunters find **evidence** that's hard to explain. Evidence is information. Ghost hunters are scientists. They collect evidence. They study evidence. They record details. They do tests.

Sometimes ghost hunters find evidence of something other than ghosts

Advice From the Field
JOE CHIN AND CHRISTINE DOWNES

Joe Chin travels the world. He stars in *Ghost Hunters International*. His sister is Christine Downes. She's also a ghost hunter. They grew up in a haunted house. They lived on the second floor of a building. The third floor was empty. They heard noises. This made them interested in hunting ghosts. They give several tips for ghost hunting. Chin said, "The more you look into the spirit world, the more happens to you. ...Whenever you leave a haunted site, make sure to say out loud, 'You may not follow me.'" Downes advises, "Always investigate in twos, never alone. Not just for safety, but for validation of what you've witnessed."

Ghost hunters are detectives. They solve mysteries. They look for clues. They ask questions.

Ghost hunters are historians. They research haunted houses. They research people who lived or died there. They use the library. They check official papers.

Ghost hunters work at night. That way human

activities won't disturb evidence. Some believe ghosts are easier to see at night.

Ghost hunters work in small groups. Too many bodies change the air. This affects the equipment, or gear. One person takes pictures. Another person films. Another person uses tools.

The best time to hunt ghosts is midnight to 4:00 a.m.
It's also best to hunt ghosts during cold, dry months.

Mists are a common type of unexplained image.

Ghost hunters use many tools. They use special cameras. These cameras take pictures in the dark. They study the pictures. They look for dark shadows. They look for glowing mists, or fogs. They look for **orbs**. Orbs are round balls of light. Some believe orbs are ghosts trying to be seen. Ghost hunters look for **vortexes**. Vortexes are swirling lights.

Ghost hunters record ghostly voices. These recordings are called **electronic voice phenomena** or EVP. **Phenomena** are experiences. Ghost hunters often don't hear the voices when recording. The voices can only be heard during a playback.

Ghost hunters take **electromagnetic field readings** or EMFs. These readings jump when a ghost is nearby.

Ghost hunters use **thermometers**. Thermometers check temperatures. Ghosts make a room cooler. Cold spots mean ghosts are near.

Ghost hunters use **thermal** equipment. Thermal means heat. Heat is a form of energy. Thermal equipment can make ghosts more visible.

Not all equipment is fancy. Some ghost hunters use talcum powder or salt. They sprinkle it around objects. They see if ghosts have moved an object. Salt also cleans the area. It takes in the ghost energy.

The purpose of equipment is to **document**, or record, evidence of ghosts.

Ghost hunters also bring flashlights,
extra batteries, and snacks.

CHAPTER 3

Ghost Hunting— Past to Present

Who are the Fox sisters? What does The Ghost Club do? What did ghost hunters do before fancy equipment?

In the 1850s, mediums were popular. People believed mediums could contact the dead.

Leah, Maggie, and Kate Fox grew up in a haunted house. Ghosts talked to them. Ghosts rapped on the walls. The Fox sisters said they could speak with the dead. They traveled around the country. They hosted events. They spoke to the dead. They were accused of being fake.

The Ghost Club was formed in 1862. It started in London. The Ghost Club promotes paranormal research. Its members didn't like people pretending to see ghosts. They didn't like fake mediums. They **exposed** them. They let the public know the mediums were fake. The club is still around today.

Famous members of the Ghost Club have included Charles Dickens (below) and Sir Arthur Conan Doyle.

Ghost hunters have been around for a long time. In the past, they didn't have fancy equipment. They just waited. They watched. They hoped to see or hear strange things.

Dr. Hans Holzer came up with the term "ghost hunter." He investigated a haunted house in Amityville. It's in New York. It was built on an Indian graveyard. The family was haunted. A family member killed other family members. Holzer took pictures. He believed the angry Indian chief possessed the killer.

In 1959, Friedrich Jurgenson recorded birds singing. He played the tape back. He heard dead family members. Since then, recorders have been important tools for EVP.

Dr. Hans Holzer also made up the term "The Other Side." This refers to where dead people live.

Ghost Hunter
KNOW THE LINGO!

Apparition: the visible appearance of a ghost

Aura: a field of energy

Crisis apparitions: ghosts that appear before a loved one right before or after dying

Crop circles: shapes that appear in large fields; believed by some to be alien communication

Demonology: study of demons

Dowsing: using rods to obtain information

Entity: an interactive ghost

Exorcism: using religious rituals to get rid of ghosts or demons

Harbinger: a ghost of the future that warns people of events

Hot spots: areas where ghost activity is concentrated

Levitate: rising in the air without help

Poltergeist: mischievous spirit, "noisy ghost"

Portal: doorway of energy where spirits may enter or exit a location

Possession: an evil ghost controlling a human body

Psychic: a person who interacts with the world with more than their five senses

Séance: a ritual to communicate with spirits of the dead

Specter: apparition

Time slips: apparitions from the past; persons or objects briefly traveling through time

Warp: location where science does not apply; distortion of time and space

CHAPTER 4

Touched by a Ghost

Why do people become ghost hunters?
What do ghost hunters hunt?

Tommy Netzband drowned in a bathtub. He was five years old. He floated to the ceiling. He saw his body in the water. His sister saved him. He's been trying to have another out-of-body experience. That's why he is a ghost hunter. He leads the San Francisco Ghost Society. He investigates the city's scariest buildings. He finds ghosts. He asks if they're willing to talk.

Many ghost hunters have their own ghost stories. Michael Rudie became interested in ghosts at five years old. He saw a ghost outside his room. Rudie investigates ghosts. He studies the history of haunted places.

Many ghost hunters have personal experience with ghosts.

WHEN ODD IS TOO ODD!

There's a ghost called "The Black Eyed Child." It has black pits instead of eyes. It was first seen in England. Many people have seen it. Lee Brickley is hunting the ghost. His aunt first saw the ghost in 1982. She heard the child cry for help. She saw the black eyes. She was scared. Some believe the ghost is linked to a Celtic tribe. The tribe is known for making blood sacrifices. Others believe people are imagining the ghost. Brickley said, "There were all kinds of weird, covert military stuff going on here during the years. There still is. Could something left behind have caused all these sightings?" He conducted many interviews. They tell the same story. Witnesses say the child giggles or calls for help. This means it's trying to trap victims. It's leading people to danger. Brickley said, "In my opinion, the Black Eyed Child seems to be some kind of demon."

Gloria Young was a nurse. She led a group of ghost hunters. Her father's ghost visited her. She smelled his smoking. She said, "A couple times, I got up to use the bathroom and I'd almost run into him. I felt the force."

Gary Galka's daughter died. He feels she's still around.

He said, "I've created over 30 different **products** for paranormal research." Products are tools.

Ghost hunters enjoy hunting for answers. They want to explain the unexplained. Brandon Alvis created the American Paranormal Research Association. He became interested in ghosts after losing two family members. He seeks to find "cold hard facts, to prove or disprove" ghosts.

Some ghost hunters become interested in ghost hunting after losing someone they love.

CHAPTER 5

Skeptics and Dangers

What is a skeptic? How do ghost hunters prove skeptics wrong? Why must ghost hunters be skeptical? What are the dangers of ghost hunting?

Skeptics don't believe in ghosts. They believe ghost reports can be explained. They believe ghost reports are just stories. They say there is no proof. Proof means the facts that prove something is real.

Ghost hunters work to prove skeptics wrong. They collect evidence. They write research papers. They use scientific methods. Finding evidence of ghosts takes hard work.

Ghost hunters are also skeptical. They need to study all the facts. Ghosts are not everywhere.

Skeptics think ghost pictures are tricks of light.

Fear is normal. It's dangerous for ghost hunters to let fear take over. Amy Bruni said, "The first thing to do is to not be afraid. We've never had a report of someone getting severely injured by a ghost."

Ghosts are not the only dangers of ghost hunting. Bruni investigated an old prison. She got lost. She ran into a person. She said, "People are so much more terrifying than ghosts." Ghost hunters should never hunt alone.

Ghost hunters can get in trouble. They should not **trespass**. Trespass means to be somewhere without permission. People think a school in Texas is haunted. People break in. The police have arrested many people. A cop said, "People think they are having some fun and looking for a ghost. They're actually breaking the law."

Trespassing is against the law.

Spotlight Biography
ELIJAH BURKE

Elijah Samuel Burke was a professional wrestler. He was on *Ghost Hunters*. He was a special guest. Before the show, he said, "Am I scared? I am absolutely not scared." He visited Waverly Hills. It's an abandoned hospital. He visited on Halloween. Thousands of people died there. It's believed to be haunted. He had several experiences. He felt cold spots. He felt something touch him. He saw a child's ball move on its own. He got scared. He screamed loudly. He ran away. He said, "All I saw was a silhouette of this shadow person. And then, he moved back. I looked back at the door. And I saw absolutely nothing out there." Shadow people are dark, human shapes. They move at night. They're a common form of ghost. Burke started as a skeptic. Now, he believes in ghosts.

DID YOU KNOW?

- Some people believe children are more likely to see ghosts. Children are more open to the paranormal.

- Dr. Gaine Cannon worked in the mountains of North Carolina. He had to visit a sick patient. He drove through a snowstorm. He couldn't find the road. He heard their family dog barking. The dog guided the car. He saved the girl. He wanted to thank the dog. He learned the dog had died several weeks earlier.

- A lot of ghostly activity takes place around mirrors. It's especially strong where two mirrors face each other. This creates reflections of reflections. It makes a tunnel of light in the glass.

- Harry Houdini was the world's greatest escape artist and stage magician. He was a skeptic. He investigated fake mediums. He exposed them.

- Ghost hunters should dress correctly. Wearing jewelry could affect pictures and videos. Light could reflect off earrings and rings. Wearing noisy shoes affects sound recordings.

- Common places to investigate ghosts are cemeteries, battlefields, churches, historic buildings, theaters, hotels, former U.S. Navy ships, crime scenes, and abandoned hospitals and prisons.

- Ghost hunters need to learn to talk to ghosts. Amy Bruni said, "Ghosts were people, too, at one point. If you don't mind it being there, let it know they're welcome in your house. And if you don't want it around, politely tell it to leave."

CONSIDER THIS!

TAKE A POSITION! Many ghost hunters have regular jobs during the day. They hunt ghosts at night or on weekends. Ghost hunters don't make a lot of money. They do it because they love it. Do you think ghost hunting is a job or a hobby? Argue your position with reasons and evidence.

SAY WHAT? Ghost hunters need to make sure they get permission to investigate haunted places. It's against the law for them to trespass in cemeteries, or graveyards. Explain the dangers of trespassing. Explain why ghost hunters need to learn about the places they investigate.

THINK ABOUT IT! Skeptics want more proof that ghosts exist. They find problems with ghost hunters' evidence. Camera flashes can cause orbs. Computers can make fake pictures. Cold spots can be caused by openings in old doors. Do you agree with the skeptics? Do you believe in paranormal investigation and research?

SEE A DIFFERENT SIDE! Ghost hunters use advanced recording equipment. Yet, there is no real proof of ghosts. Marley Gibson, Patrick Burns, and Dave Schrader wrote a book about ghost hunting. They said, "You cannot scientifically prove ghosts exist—no matter how awesome a photograph you took. It's always open to other interpretations in the eyes of the scientist." What does proof mean to a ghost hunter? What does proof mean to a skeptic?

LEARN MORE

PRIMARY SOURCES

Ghost Hunters (Syfy Channel, TV show): www.syfy.com/ghosthunters
Paranormal State (A&E Channel, TV show): www.aetv.com/paranormal-state/video

SECONDARY SOURCES

Gibson, Marley, Patrick Burns, and Dave Schrader. *The Other Side: A Teen's Guide to Ghost Hunting and the Paranormal.* Boston: Houghton Mifflin Harcourt, 2009.
Martin, Michael. *Ghost Hunters.* Mankato, MN: Capstone Press, 2012.
Owen, Ruth. *Ghosts and Other Spirits of the Dead.* New York: Bearport Publishing, 2013.

WEB SITES

Atlantic Paranormal Society: www.the-atlantic-paranormal-society.com
American Paranormal Research Association: http://apraparanormal.com
Association for the Scientific Study of Anomalous Phenomena: www.assap.ac.uk

GLOSSARY

document (DAHK-yuh-muhnt) to record something that happened

electromagnetic field readings (i-lek-troh-mag-NEH-tik FEELD REED-ingz) records of movements in Earth's magnetic fields taken by a machine

electronic voice phenomena (i-lek-TRAH-nik VOIS fuh-NAH-muh-nuh) machine recordings of ghost voices that were not heard at the time of recording

evidence (EV-ih-duhns) information, data

exposed (ik-SPOZED) revealed as fake

guardian (GAHR-dee-uhn) a guard, protector

hauntings (HAWNT-ingz) when a ghost occupies a location, or bothers a person

mediums (MEE-dee-uhmz) people who talk to ghosts or the dead

orbs (ORBZ) glowing balls of light sometimes connected to ghostly activity

paranormal (par-uh-NOR-muhl) anything to do with unexplained events

phenomena (fuh-NAH-muh-nuh) experiences

products (PRAH-duhkts) things people buy and use

skeptics (SKEP-tiks) people who don't believe in ghosts

thermal (THUR-muhl) heat

thermometers (thur-MAH-mi-turz) tools that measure temperature

trespass (TRES-pas) to enter a place without permission

vortexes (VOR-teks-ez) whirling masses of light connected to ghostly activity

INDEX

ABOUT THE AUTHOR

Dr. Virginia Loh-Hagan is an author, university professor, former classroom teacher, and curriculum designer. She totally believes in ghosts. She loves ghost stories. She lives in San Diego with her very tall husband and very naughty dogs. To learn more about her, visit www.virginialoh.com.